D0636891

USING THIS BOOK

*One of the best ways of helping children to learn to read is by reading stories to them and with them. This way they learn what **reading** is, and they will gradually come to recognise many words, and begin to read for themselves.*

First, grown-ups read the story on the left-hand pages aloud to the child.

You can reread the story as often as the child enjoys hearing it. Talk about the pictures as you go.

Later the child is encouraged to read the words under the pictures on the right-hand page.

The pages at the back of the book will give you some ideas for helping your child to read.

British Library Cataloguing in Publication Data

McCullagh, Sheila K.
    Tim turns green. — (Puddle Lane reading programme. Stage 1; v. 12)
    1. Readers — 1950-
    I. Title   ·II. Smith, Sheila   III. Series
    428.6
    ISBN 0-7214-0911-3

First edition

Published by Ladybird Books Ltd Loughborough Leicestershire UK
Ladybird Books Inc Lewiston Maine 04240 USA

© Text and layout SHEILA McCULLAGH MCMLXXXVI
© In publication LADYBIRD BOOKS LTD MCMLXXXVI

All rights reserved. No part of this publication may be reproduced, stored in a retrieval system, or transmitted in any form or by any means, electronic, mechanical, photo-copying, recording or otherwise, without the prior consent of the copyright owners.

Tim
turns green

written by SHEILA McCULLAGH
illustrated by SHEILA SMITH

This book belongs to:

Judith Katrie Forbes

aged 5

Ladybird Books

Little Tim Catchamouse ran
up the roof of the old house,
till he came to the skylight window.

Tim ran up the roof.

The window was open.

Tim looked down into the room below.

He knew that a magician
lived in the house,
but the room was empty.
The Magician wasn't there.

Tim looked down.

A long pole was leaning up against
the window. Tim climbed down
the pole to the floor.

He ran over to the Magician's chair.

Tim ran
to the chair.

He jumped up on to the chair,
and looked around.

The chair was close to a big table.

Tim jumped up
on to the chair.

Tim jumped up on to the table.

Tim jumped up
on to the table.

A jar was standing
on the table.

Tim ran across to the jar.
He put his paws on the top
of the jar, and sniffed a big sniff.
Something inside the jar
smelt very good.

Tim ran to the jar.

The jar fell over.

Some green mice fell out
on to the table.
The mice were made of sugar.

16

The jar fell over.

Tim was hungry.

He looked at the sugar mice.
They made him feel hungrier and
hungrier.

"Magicians don't eat mice,"
Tim said to himself.
"Cats eat mice. The Magician must
have left them here for me."

So he ate a green mouse.
It tasted very good.

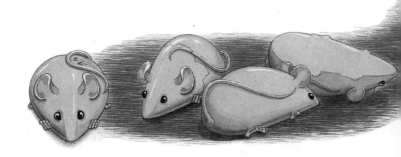

Tim ate a mouse.

He was very hungry,
so he ate two more sugar mice.
He was just going to eat another,
when he looked across at
the wall of the room.

Tim ate two mice.

There was a mirror on the wall.
Tim could see himself
in the mirror.

He looked at the mirror —
and gave a loud cry.

"Miaow!" cried Tim.

He could see a little cat
in the mirror. But the little cat
had turned green!

Tim saw a green cat.

Tim looked down at his paws.
His paws were green!

Tim looked down at
his paws.
His paws were green.

He ran round and round on the table,
trying to look at his tail.
His tail had turned green!

"Miaow!" cried Tim. "Miaow!"

Tim looked at his tail.
His tail was green.

The door of the room opened,
and the Magician came in.

He took one look at Tim,
and he began to laugh.

"You bad little cat," he cried.
"You've been eating
my magic green sugar mice."

the Magician

"**Please** turn me back again!"
cried Tim. "**Please** make me black!
I didn't think you'd mind me
eating a mouse.
And I was so hungry."

He looked at his green paws, and
he cried.

Tim looked at
his green paws.

"Don't cry," said the Magician.
"I ought to leave you green,
just to teach you a lesson.
But I won't. I'll turn you
back to your own colour again."

He looked at Tim.

"Green cat, turn back —
green cat, turn black!" he cried.

And he snapped his fingers.

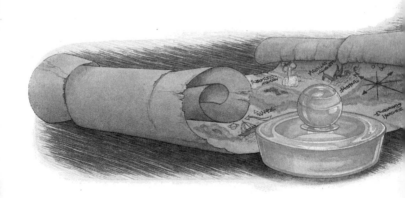

Tim, the green cat

There was a flash of green fire —
and Tim was a little black cat again.

Tim, the black cat

"Next time you eat my magic green mice,
I shall leave you all green,"
said the Magician.

"I won't eat them again," said Tim.
"I thought you had left them there
for me."

"Well, I hadn't," said the Magician.

He looked at Tim.

"But I know you didn't mean to be bad.
You can come again,
if you'd like to," he said.

The Magician
looked at Tim.

Tim climbed up the pole,
and out of the window.
He ran down the roof
and jumped on to the tree.
He climbed down the tree
to the garden.

He didn't feel **quite** happy, until
he was safely back home.

"But I will go back,"
he said to himself.
"I won't eat any more green mice,
but I'll go back and see
the Magician."

Tim climbed
down the tree.

When you are sure that the child can read these successfully, ask him to read the words to you. Let him look at the pictures.

green

black

cat

a black cat

a green cat

40

a green cat

a black cat

a green cat

a green mouse

a black mouse

Now cover the pictures, and see if the child can still read the words, uncovering the pictures one by one, so that he can see for himself if he is right.

Notes for the parent/teacher

When you have read the story, go back to the beginning. Look at each picture and talk about it, pointing to the caption below, and reading it aloud yourself.

Run your finger along under the words as you read, so that the child learns that reading goes from left to right. (You needn't say this in so many words. Children learn many useful things about reading by just reading with you, and it is often better to let them learn by experience, rather than by explanation.) When you next go through the book, encourage the child to read the words and sentences under the illustrations.

Don't rush in with the word before he* has time to think, but don't leave him struggling for too long. Always encourage him to feel that he is reading successfully, praising him when he does well, and avoiding criticism.

Now turn back to the beginning, and print the child's name in the space on the title page, using ordinary, not capital letters. Let him watch you print it: this is another useful experience.

*Children enjoy hearing the same story many times. Read this one as often as the child likes hearing it. The more opportunities he has of looking at the illustrations and **reading** the captions with you, the more he will come to recognise the words. Don't worry if he **remembers** rather than **reads** the captions. This is a normal stage in learning.*

If you have a number of books, let him choose which story he would like to have again.

**Footnote:* In order to avoid the continual "she or he", "her or him", the child is referred to in this book as "he". However, the stories are equally appropriate for girls and boys.

Puddle Lane Reading Programme   Stage 1

There are several books at this Stage about the same characters. All the books at each Stage are separate stories and are written at the same reading level.

There are more stories about Tim and Tessa and the Magician in these books:

Stage 1

Tessa and Tim

the Magician